THIS BOOK BELONGS TO

____

____

Table of contents

INTRODUCTION

Hello,

My name is Mr. Socksolopomialadaschiz.
But you can call me by my nickname

Mr. Socks.

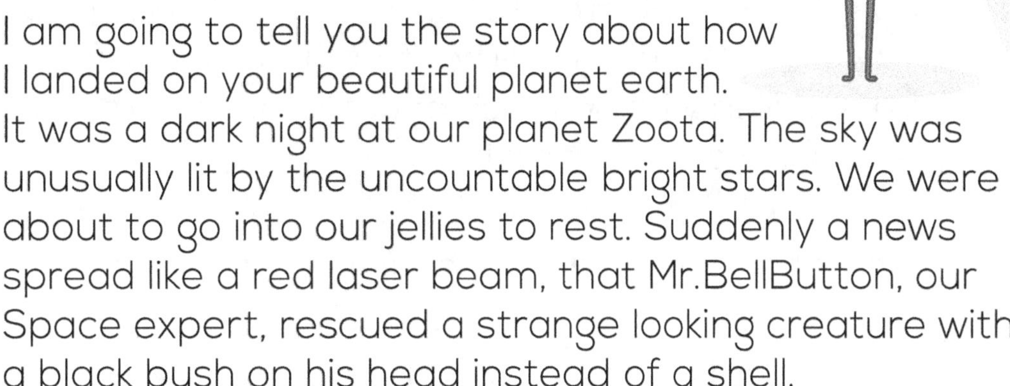

I am going to tell you the story about how I landed on your beautiful planet earth.
It was a dark night at our planet Zoota. The sky was unusually lit by the uncountable bright stars. We were about to go into our jellies to rest. Suddenly a news spread like a red laser beam, that Mr.BellButton, our Space expert, rescued a strange looking creature with a black bush on his head instead of a shell.

According to Mr.BellButton, he was lost in space with a strangely small pink shuttle. Everybody lined up to get a glimpse of the strange creature. When it came out of the rescue station, it started making weird noises, at which Mr. BellButton told us that this is his way of communicating.

Mr. BellButton called Mr. Mosomo, the language expert to interpret. According to Mr. Mosomo, the new creature was saying this:

Well, I don't want to brag and all but at this, everybody turned towards me, as I am the awesomest storyteller of all times. I have been narrating stories since I was created and people come from farther planets just to learn the art. So, long story short, I was then sent to Earth to bring laughter and happiness through teaching the art of storytelling to the children of your beautiful planet. The fun thing is, that your planet is already filled with so much beauty and love that you just have to look closely and observe!

So let's begin the fun ride and play some games!

WARM UP EXERCISES

Guess work:

Jonathan's birthday is approaching. He has sensed his family preparing a huge surprise for him. His younger sister leaked the news that he might get five things he has always wanted. He is interested in astronomy and space. Guess what is in the gift boxes hidden in his mother's closet.

1. _______________

2. _______________

3. _______________

4. _______________

5. _______________

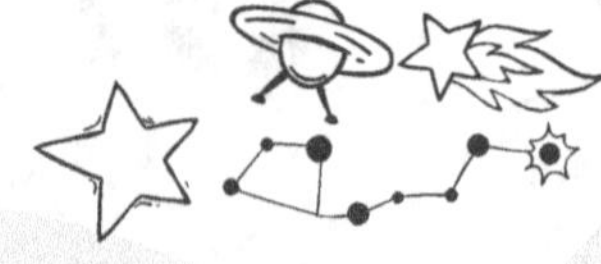

Describe the setting shown here.

You can write about the weather, living things, greenery, colors, objects and overall feel of the picture.

____

____

____

____

Describe the action

You can write about their thoughts and feelings when describing the action!

____

____

____

____

____

____

Describe yourself by answering these questions:

What is it that you most likely want to do in your relaxed time?

What do you find odd about this world and its people?

What interests you most about nature?

Who is your favorite person and why?

Imagine and ask yourself:

Imagine you are camping outside with your family. You wake up early in the morning when everyone else is asleep.

Write down what you hear, how the weather is, how you feel and what is it that you see.

____

____

____

psst, listen carefully and don't ignore the snoring sounds

____

Write a diary for a single day

Write a dairy of a strange wizard who turns into a cat to spy on his neighbors.

Guess what they are thinking.

Pick three and write an absurd story

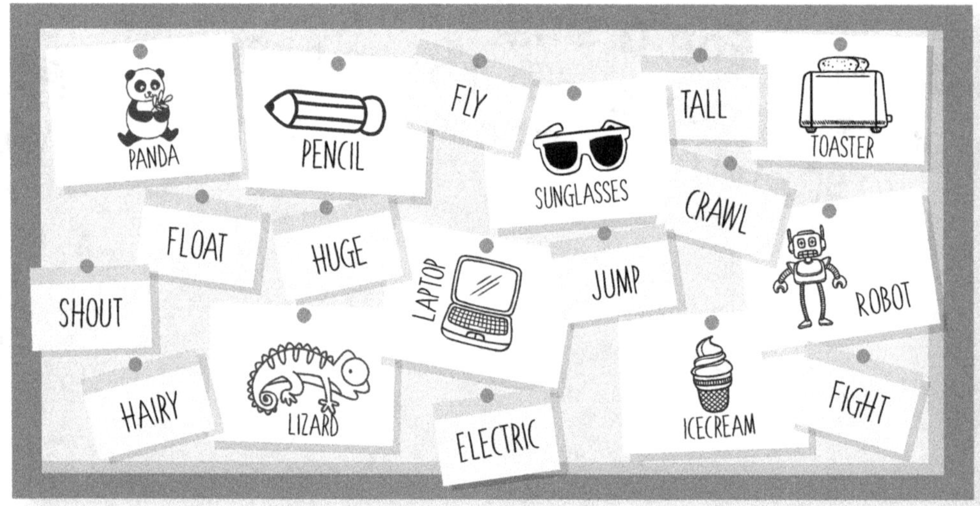

Example:
Carrot+rabbit+ flying=
A story about a rabbit fying on a carrot.

Draw here

CHARACTER DESIGN

Characters are the basic unit of a story. They add interest and connect the reader to your story. Here are the steps to create and write your character wisely:

Step 1. Choose your character from any category you like.

Example: Unusual, usual, alien, human, animal, monster, machine or whatever comes to your mind.

Don't limit yourself, it can be something so extraordinary as food

____

Example: Huge, small, tall, short, hair, clothes, limbs, colors or anything interesting that catches the eye..

Step 2. Think about what they look like!

____

____

Step 3. Make up their personality.

Example: Likes, dislikes, attitude, mood, occupation, routine, pet..

Design with us!
Follow the steps mentioned above. Draw your character here.

____

____

____

Step 4. Give them a title/name.

Example: Mr, Mrs, Sir, Lady, Doctor, Captain, Professor, Name.

____

____

Describe these characters

Name: _____________________

Description: _____________________

____

Name: _____________________

Description: _____________________

____

Name: _____________________

Description: _____________________

____

Name: _____________________

Description: _____________________

____

Draw lines to match each describing word with an object to create interesting characters. Then draw one of the most interesting ones that you created.

Match

Rude	Octopus
Slimy	Alien
Lazy	Monster
Colorful	Banana
Fragile	Kid
Athletic	Rose
Savage	Mountain
Wrinkled	Jacket
Dangerous	Car

Create

Plot Plan

Once the character and setting are in place, the sequence in the story is usually this:

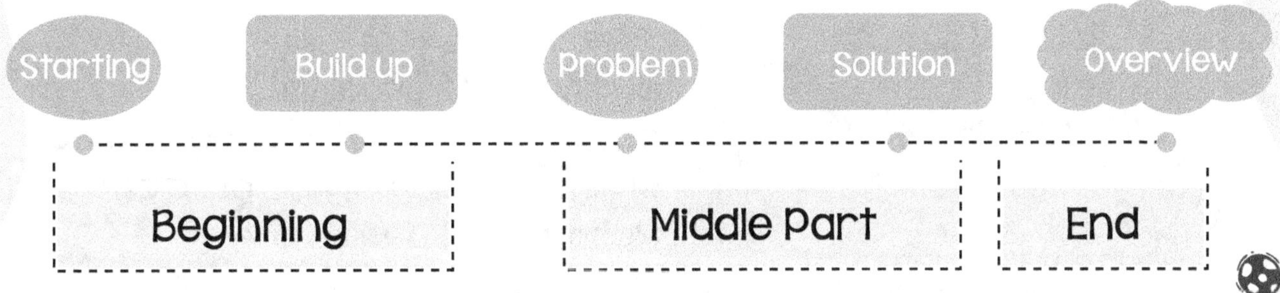

Lets review each component of the story and do some exercises along the way.

Beginning

The beginning of any text or story is important for the reader to keep on reading and be interested in that text/story. As a writer, you should be extra creative with how you begin your story. Here are some tips for you.

1. You can begin with the **usual** and the most easy words, 'Once upon a time' or 'Once'.

2. It's not compulsory to start with the above-mentioned words. Although mostly these are useful words, keep in mind there are other options too. You can start with describing the **setting** of your story.

For example, 'In a cave of the blue mountain, far from the village, lived an old woman....'

3. A story can also begin with someone's **speech**.

For example, "Hey young lad!", shouted the angry old man as I dashed out of his sight.

4. Rarely, you will find a story beginning with a **dramatic event**. It is useful to immediately catch readers interest especially if it's an action story.

For example, BAM! Our car collided with the tree and I could see the dark smoke rising.

5. **Adjectives** or describing words add interest to the beginning. For example, a tall guy with an orange hat might sound more interesting than just 'a guy'. Why? Because you have made them enter the world of imagination!!

Build up

Build up is just an expansion of the beginning. It usually consists of details of characters and setting or the starting of the problem. Remember! details are important.

Like, for example, if you are writing about a guy on a mission to search for his lost sister; you can start by introducing the guy and then adding details about his personality, routine, pets or whatever, so that the reader feels like they know him.

NOW, LET'S DO SOME FUN PRACTICE!!

- TURN A BORING BEGINNING INTO AN INTERESTING ONE

There lived a smart kid in a farmhouse who liked to invent things.

Your story can also start with a loud sound from his failed invention!

- THE MIDDLE OF THE STORY IS GIVEN. WRITE AN APPROPRIATE BEGINNING.

...But the problem was that she hated her little brother, who would take away all the attention and time of their parents. Sometimes she wondered if she was actually nice or just pretending. She didn't feel like being polite and sweet with Lucas when nobody was watching. Strangely, Lucas was very well-behaved with her. She had to struggle with finding issues to be crossed at him, at which he would immediately comply with her wishes.

You can include: girl's name & her personality. Introduce the brother, Lucas

Middle

The middle of the story is usually the part where the real problem in the story is mentioned. Some tips to write an engaging middle part are:

- Add a lot of drama and action. **Exaggerate** stuff if need be.

- **Don't always use 'said',** when writing about someone's speech. It makes the story monotonous. You can use shout, yelled, called, groaned, cried e.t.c.

- Usually in a story, there is a problem and then at the end, we write about the solution found by the characters. But there can be **multiple problems and solutions**. This way your middle part can be made more exciting.

- Don't just state all the events in a boring sequence rather **describe in detail the feelings, settings and action** along the way, as if you have lived the story by yourself.

So that the reader also feels like he is actually experiencing the story.

LET'S PRACTICE!

A story plot is given with the beginning and the end mentioned, write an interesting and adventurous middle part.

You can write about his adventures, more than one problem and their solutions.

THERE WAS A PRINCE IN SEARCH OF A BLUE FLOWER FOR HER MOTHER, THE QUEEN; WHO HAD FALLEN SICK SINCE THE LAST LEAF OF AUTUMN HAD FALLEN.

IN THE END, HE FINDS THE FLOWER AND THE QUEEN STARTS TO RECOVER. SHE IS PROUD OF HER SON.

Ending

The end of a story is responsible for leaving a lasting impression on the reader. To write an ending, keep these few tips in mind and you're good to go:

1. Stories often end with the problem being solved or the plan working out.

2. At the end, don't forget to wrap up the story of each of the characters you have mentioned and all the problems that arose.

It can be annoying for the reader to be left guessing about one of the main characters.

3. It's not necessary to keep the ending happy or to make the reader happy. Many famous stories have sad endings.

PRACTICE TIME!

Write a different ending to the famous story

Gingerbread man.

A LITTLE OLD MAN AND A LITTLE OLD WOMAN STAYED IN A COTTAGE. ONE DAY, THE WOMAN MADE A GINGERBREAD MAN FOR DINNER. SHE DECORATED THE GINGERBREAD MAN WITH EYES MADE OF CURRANTS AND BUTTONS MADE OF CHERRIES. BUT WHEN SHE TOOK OUT GINGERBREAD MAN FROM THE OVEN, HE JUMPED OUT AND RAN AWAY.

THE OLD WOMAN AND HER HUSBAND RAN AFTER HIM BUT THE GINGERBREAD MAN WAS TOO FAST FOR THEM. NEITHER THE PIG, NOR THE COW, NOR THE HORSE WHO FOLLOWED, COULD OUTRUN GINGERBREAD MAN. NOW, THE GINGERBREAD MAN CAME TO A RIVER AND DIDN'T KNOW HOW TO CROSS IT. A SLY FOX CAME UP TO HIM AND OFFERED TO HELP HIM CROSS THE RIVER. THE FOX ASKED HIM TO SIT ON HIS TAIL BUT THE GINGERBREAD MAN BEGAN TO GET WET. THEN THE FOX TOLD HIM TO SIT ON HIS BACK AND FINALLY ON HIS NOSE.

NO SOONER DID GINGERBREAD MAN SIT ON THE FOX'S NOSE, THAT THE SLY FOX TOSSED HIM AND GOBBLED HIM UP.

This is kind of a sad ending, you can change it into a happy one, if you like.

PROMPTS

BEGIN!

Magic Pencil

Daisy was disappointed with all the birthday gifts she received. Even Aunt Margaret, who had previously set a record of giving the most interesting gifts, had given a lousy pencil. Daisy impulsively started to scribble with it. Magically, the pencil started writing the exact same words that she was thinking. Daisy has a pencil that could write the thoughts of the person holding it.

Lousy: terrible

A Secret Power

Linda could see behind the walls. She never felt like telling this to anybody. She just had this power since always. It was totally normal for her. As she grew up and realized how strange this was, she still didn't mention for the fear of being labeled as the odd one.

The Untold Story

I'm your favorite toy/object, write my story from start to end. Write about how I was made. How I landed in your hands. What is going to be my possible future?

Draw here!

The Giant who stopped the Rain

There was a giant who used to get really scared whenever it rained. One day he decided to stop the rain by making a huge ladder that reached the clouds. He went up and stopped the rain, but people got angry.

Draw here!

The Unicorn with Socks on

Today Ethan was sick and at home with his mum, wandering around the house. He went to his backyard when he found a magical unicorn standing with socks on. The unicorn could talk also. Ethan was surprised.

How will he react? What will they do together?

Draw here!

Wandering: *Roaming*

Lost in the Dollhouse

She always wanted a real size doll house. This time, the whole family decided to contribute for one big gift instead of multiple small ones, and get her dream dollhouse. She was thrilled beyond words and went inside of it. Strangely, it appeared even bigger than her house and after a few minutes, she was lost inside it. It was a magic doll house but how will she get out?

Draw here!

Thrilled: Delighted   **Contribute:** Give

The Revenge of the Superhero

In my opinion, being a superhero and having to hide it, is actually worse than having no powers at all. Since I have started high school, I have been constantly bullied by the seniors but no, I cannot take revenge due to 'the rules' of the superheroes. But, one day I am going to have them pay back.

Who set the rules and why? How is he going to take revenge? Will he break the rules?

Revenge: *tit for tat*

Brocolli's Mission

Hi, I'm an angry broccoli. I am extremely upset by the image people, especially kids, have associated me with. I am delicious and most people would eat me if not for the biasness. I am on a mission to change this idea about me.

Write about the broccoli's plan and whether it's a successful one or not? The broccoli can make posters, ads and other resources as well in your story.

Draw here!

Biasness: *inclination to a particular side*

Turning into a Superhero

Olivia is a shy girl. She is contacted by the council of superheroes secretly and asked to select a super power for herself. She has to promise that she won't be revealing her powers to anyone except for one person only.

Which power will she select? Who will she share the news with?

Revealing: *giving away or disclosing*

Under to Rule of the Sloths

It was a matter of few weeks that the whole planet was taken over by the sloths. For some reason, they had learned the art of speaking. They are extremely slow but very smart. The humans have to follow their orders.

What will the world look like? Will you be comfortable in such a place? Will the systems start to collapse eventually?

Draw here!

Collapse: *fall down*   **Eventually:** *in time*

The Twisted Tongue

Suddenly you start speaking a foreign language instead of your mother tongue. The people around you have no idea what you're talking about and you are unable to switch back to your language.

What would you do? How will it get better?

Finding her Voice again

A strange witch with purple teeth, at the bus stop took away your ability to sing because you accidentally stepped on her toe. You have a singing competition in a week. Find her and ask for a cure.

How do you find her? Does she agree? What are her conditions to give you your talent back?

Draw here!

The Real Money Plant

Alice had recently developed an interest in plants. Her mother promised to buy her one plant every month. This month she bought a money plant. The pot had strange writing and symbols on it. After a few days the plant actually started producing money, but the only problem was that the money (currency) was of another country.

What did she do with the money?

Developed: *grew*

Fly away William

William was born in a family of witches and wizards. They were nice people and hated dishonesty. William was turned into a bird as a punishment for lying to his father. He was told that the only way he would be turned back into a human was if he flew all the way to the other side of the world.

Write about his journey, the challenges and the solution.

Q **Dishonesty:** lying

The Anger Stare

Ellas has a weird condition. Whenever she stares a person or an object with anger, that person or the object falls down.

Cure: heal

A Sweet House.

There is a family that lives in a house made of biscuits, if they eat even a bit of it, the house will collapse.

Write about their daily experiences.

Draw here!

Collapse: *Fall in*

Luna and the Sleeping Dragon

Luna was wandering in the backyard and saw a sleeping dragon.

Does she make friends with him? Is he a dangerous one or a friendly one?

Draw here!

Conference of the Planets

There is a meeting of all the planets, and earth is as usual late and full of excuses.

What is being discussed? What are earth's excuses? Does it get any punishment? What is the punishment?

The Invisible Kid

Adam was afraid initially because nobody was responding to him since he had worn the new t-shirt this morning that he found in the garage sale. After an hour at school though, he realized he had turned invisible and now he was planning to enjoy this!

____

____

____

____

____

____

____

____

____

____

____

Initially: _at first_   **Responding:** _answering_

The Watch that did not Exist

Hanna boasted about having a watch that was hundred years old and had cool functions. But she had lied. She doesn't own such a watch. Now the teacher asks her to bring that watch for an experiment next week. What functions did she say the watch has? Does she admit that she lied? What is everybody's reaction?

The Revenge

It all started when Sara stuck her chewed gum in my locker because obviously she felt jealous of my performance at the singing club. I had never felt more nervous and elevated at the same time while performing and then winning the prize. But this bullying was ruining everything. I had to take revenge.

Elevated: *raised*   **Revenge:** *tit for tat*

Lizy's Struggles

Lizy is the smartest and youngest student among all the eighth graders, plus she is petite and tiny. Write about the struggles and attitudes she has to endure. Does she find peace with her class fellows and make friends?

Petite: *small*   **Endure:** *face, suffer or handle*

The leaked video on YouTube

My brother is the worst brother anyone could ever have. He played a prank on me and without telling me, recorded it in a video. And now it's uploaded on YouTube with all the kids in my school watching and laughing.

Write about how you react and control the situation? Who supports you? Is your brother ashamed?

Prank: *trick/joke*

Competing for the Lead Role.

Getting the lead role in the drama club was Tom's biggest dream. Yesterday, he got the news that he will be getting one. He took his time to get ready for the first rehearsal session, singing happily. As soon as they are seated in the club room, the teacher announces a change in plan that Walter will be the new lead role and Tom will be an extra in the play.

Does he compromise or fight for it?

Q **Lead role:** hero **Extra** *(in a drama)* : additional role

The Rejected Genius

Stefan was always trying new things and reading books too advanced for a boy his age. Mathematics and Science were his favorite subjects, but he lacked in other areas like Literature, Music and above all, behavior. After multiple warnings he was kicked out of the school.

My Friend's forgotten Phone

Last night Isabel came to my home for a joint school project. We had dinner together and then she left, forgetting her phone in my bedroom. Her phone is not locked and I am curious about the conversations between our common friend Danna and her. Should I spy or not? What will I find? Do I pull a prank on her? Do I bribe her?

Spy: *see, notice or detect*

The Untold Trouble

Nathan always used to score highest grades in our class, but now he can't seem to focus and gets an F in most papers. The teachers have talked to him to find out the reason behind this sudden change, but he doesn't give any hint. He has started acting strangely too. Everyone is expecting me to find out as I am his closest friend.

Focus: *fix one's attention*

The Forgotten Geography Project.

For the whole week Susan had been busy with the geography project. It was the first time she had gathered the courage to participate, due to her favorite teacher Ms. Natasha's insistence. She was so lost in her thoughts that she forgot her project model in the bus and hopped out of it.

Gathered: collected   **Insistence:** demand

Underdressed by mistake

Anthony couldn't think of a worse situation than which he was in. He had come to a Grand event arranged by the five schools jointly. Everyone was dressed up to their finest but he had worn flip flops by mistake.

My team's Resentment

It was school decoration activity week at our school. Me and my team were in charge of decorating the walls of the first floor. I was the team leader. We worked really hard and I made sure no one was left behind. Our floor decoration won the first prize but somehow during the prize distribution, only I got all the praise while it was a team effort. I could sense my team's resentment. What should I do now?

Praise: *congratulate* **Resentment:** *bitterness*

The Lost Calculator

For a school project, Thomas has promised the teacher to bring his father's antique calculator tomorrow. All the arrangements for the project have been made. But now he can't seem to find it. His father is away on a business trip and his mother's phone has broken. What does he do?

____

____

____

____

____

____

____

____

____

____

____

Q **Antique:** _very old_

A Painful Competition

The sports teacher won't let Evelyn participate in the swimming competition if he gets to know about the bruise she got in her leg last night. The competition winner will recieve cash prize and she needs the money for her homeless friend Alan. Does she hide it or tell her sports teacher? Does she receive the cash prize in the end?

Q **Bruise:** *injury*

My Rude Friend

Peter was the new kid in our class. He was looked down upon by everyone else because of his dressing sense, but for some reason I connected quite well with him. He was amazing in arts and at writing essays. We used to share ideas and discuss novels. The only thing was that bothered me was his rudeness.

Antique: very old

The Mysterious Butler

Benjamin always suspected the strange ways of the big and jolly butler. There was this rumour that he disappeared on every third wednesday of the month, around midnight. Benjamin couldn't resist anymore and followed the big guy, only to watch him vanish behind a strange door in the corner of the garden wall that was hidden behind the old tree. Benjamin is curious to find more.

Butler: *a man servant*   **rumour:** *gossip*

The Wailing Well

Blake was visiting his aunt and uncle who lived by the countryside, in a big farm. There was a well near the farm where kids would gather around and play. But today they could hear a wailing sound from the well, too soft for a human and too shrill for an animal.

Who was it? What will the kids do?

Draw here!

Shrill: *sharp*

The Mysterious Person at the Zoo

Zoo is Amelia's favorite place. Unlike most kids, she likes to visit the zoo again and again and could spend hours looking at the animals. But today she saw a strange person at the zoo, feeding the animals a strange pill, and the animals would fall asleep within the next minute. How does she alert the authorities?

Draw here!

Authorities: *officials*

The Treasure Box in the Sea

Elijah went snorkeling with his family friends. They went quite far and deep. Suddenly Elijah got a glimpse of something shiny in the ground. He went closer and dug a bit and came across an old treasure box.

What did he do next? What was inside the box? What will he do with all the stuff inside it?

Draw here!

Glimpse: *peek*

The Secret Passage

Ella was prohibited to go to the nearby public park by her parents. She had always heard strange rumors about the place. Recently it had been sealed by the authorities due to some incident nobody was telling her about. Last night, she dreamed of a secret passage in the public park where a treasure is hidden.

Did she go? Was her dream true?

Draw here!

Sealed: shut   **Incident:** event

Investigating Grandpa's Robbery

Henry's grandpa is suspected of robbery. He is sure he didn't do it as he was with Henry at the time of robbery, but the CCTV footage of robbery shows grandpa's face. Henry investigates to find proof.

Suspected: doubted   **Investigating:** look into   **Footage:** video tape

The Surprise Supper

Cooking was Lily's favorite hobby. She decided to surprise everyone by preparing a three-course meal, while everyone was away. Write about her menu, ingredients, struggle, chaos and finally her family's reaction.

Her experiment can or cannot be successful

Three-course meal:
meal that consists of three parts

Our Secret Party

Mum and dad had been planning to go on a dinner next week and leave the two of us alone at home. My brother, Clark and I had started planning a party for our school fellows in their absence.

Trouble on the Mountains

After months of planning, the two families finally set out for a fun trip to the valley behind the green mountains. The van was filled with laughter and energy. As it traveled on the narrow mountain roads the driver suddenly pulled the breaks. A large tree had fallen on the road and blocked their way. Turning back was equally impossible as they were already short of fuel.

Broken Car on the Highway

Leo always hated nighttime drives on the highway. But he couldn't avoid this one as the whole family had to attend the funeral of a close relative in the nearby town. Suddenly, he felt the car getting slow and eventually it stopped.

Who will fix their car? Does something unusual happen with them before the help arrives? Do they reach home safely?

The lost Twins

Joshua and Ethen were twins. They were camping by the forest with ten families. They decided to explore the place. But after some time they realized they had come too far in the forest and now they are lost.

How do they survive? What troubles do they have to go through? How are they found?

Family Fun

Lost in the Storage Area

Tracy was in the supermarket with her parents and her younger brother. She asked her mother if she could get the eggs and bread from the other aisle. On her way she found a strange big door which read 'Storage Area'. Out of curiosity she entered that area and started exploring it. Finally, she realized that she is lost in that storage area.

Write about her panic. How did she calm herself down? How did she find her way out? What actions did her mother take? How do they finally reunite?

Vast: *huge*

The Disastrous Thanksgiving Party

Mom had invited twenty people on this thanksgiving and made all the arrangements a few days earlier. I had never seen her so enthusiastic. However, on the day of the party she burnt the turkey she had made using her special recipe. I knew I had to do something. I finally managed to save the day. How?

My Sick Sister

My sister Leona is sick with a severe disease that needs a huge amount of money for treatment. I cannot see her and our parent's struggle like this. I have to find a job for at least four hours a week and put in some bucks for her surgery.

How do you search for work? Which job will you land on? Will your sister get better in the end?

Severe: *serious*

Lisa's Baby Sister

Lisa has heard kids in her class wishing for a baby sibling, but she never understood the feeling. In fact, being the only child she hated the idea of sharing her parents with someone else, let alone with a sister, who would be just like her and could replace her. But here she was standing in the hospital room, watching this new baby sister for the first time.

Losing the Dog

Lucas thought it was unfair that Ava was allowed to take the dog for a walk although Ava was only two years older. Today he insisted continuously until finally his mother gave in. He excitedly took the dog for a walk to the park. At the park, Lucas got distracted for a few minutes and the dog ran away! Now Lucas is worried because he can't seem to find him.

🔍 **Insisted:** *demanded/ pressed*

Surprise for Dad

Since mom passed away, Dad had become lonely. Still, he would work non-stop for the kids. Noah felt sorry for dad, he wanted to give him a break. Together with his younger sister Ira, they decided to collect money to gift dad a spa voucher.

How do they collect money? What is Dad's reaction? How did it go?

Voucher: *ticket*

Kingdom of the White Tigress of North

The official meeting of the jungle is chaired by the white tigress of the north. The issue under discussion had filled the animals of the kingdom with anger. A solution must be devised, roared the lions. We cannot take it any longer, barked the fox.

What is the problem? And what solution do they agree upon?

Draw here!

The Mouse with a Large Appetite

You are a mouse with a large appetite. You are constantly hungry and get kicked out of all the pantries and cupboards containing delicious food. You are sick of this life. Write about your adventures and a plan to get out of this situation.

Appetite: *hunger*

Owl's Lost Wisdom

Every animal in the southern jungle relied mostly on advice of the wise owl. One day, the owl boasted about his wisdom in front of the poor rabbit. The next morning, the wisdom of the owl was lost. Now the owl is on a mission to restore his wisdom.

Draw here!

Cute Hamster or a Naughty Mouse

Zoe took a stand against her family to bring a cute little hamster into her house. Turns out it is actually a very naughty mouse and you are sick of it now.

The Queen of Sea

Tess considered the sea as her best friend. She loved nothing more than a trip to the beach and could spend hours over there. Today she went under a sea wearing the special gear. She saw a grand entrance and went inside. She had entered the underwater secret world. Soon she was noticed and was made the Queen because of the strange rules they had.

Draw here!

Stuck with the Lion

Liam, the lion tamer, had been doing his job for the past ten years. He was responsible for the meals of the lion that belonged to a rich billionaire. One morning he went inside the cage to keep the food and got stuck in the lion's cage for the whole day.

What will happen when the lion is hungry again?

Draw here!

Tamer: *trainer*

The Pet Swap

There was a cat and the dog who were friends with each other. One day they decided to exchange their personalities for a day by asking the weird witch. Talk about the surprises they give to their owners.

Zebras took the colors

One day suddenly all the zebras are gone from the jungle and everything is black and white. How do the animals bring the zebras and the colors back?

Draw here!

In Search of the Lost Diamond

They set out to find the missing diamond of their grandma's ring. They packed with them the secret letter from the mystery girl. In the letter she had written that she had seen the bright diamond in a wicked man's corner closet, continents away from grandma.

Wicked: evil

Attack of the Giant Birds

The world is going to be attacked by giant birds from another planet. Frank is the only one who can save it. Write about the powers and resources he has to stop them.

A Wise man's Cure for the Pandemic

There is a strange pandemic taking over the world. Whoever is affected by it gets green pimples all over his body. The wise old man from the caves knocked the door of the castle to tell about the solution that he has found in the mountains which are surrounded with danger. You volunteer to make the trip.

Write about your struggles and endeavors.

Draw here!

Q **Pandemic:** *a disease that spreads worldwide*   **Endeavors:** *to do something with effort*

Travelling in the Wrong Plane

Nathan was traveling to New York with his family. At the airport, just before the boarding time was about to end, he had to go to the bathroom and couldn't stand in the line. He told his mama and rushed to the bathroom. On his way back, he hastily stood in the wrong queue for another plane. The person on duty mistakenly thought that he was with the family in front of him. On the plane he realized he is going to Chicago.

What happens then? What does his mama do? What experiences and troubles are waiting for him? How do they find him and meet safely in the end?

Draw here!

Hastily: *hurriedly*

The Prince's Adventure

Prince Sebastian hated being a prince. He would sneak into a public place and observe the normal kids behaving as carefree individuals and wished he had that freedom. He sets out for an adventurous journey with some money and a small bag. Little did he know he would be regretting this decision.

Draw here!

Regret: *be sorry about*

Tourism at its best

Uncle Fredrick was rich and the best uncle anyone could ever have. He was so pleased with the collection of poems that I had written that he offered me a plane ticket for any country I would like to visit, with an adult ofcourse.

Draw here!

Tourism: *travel*

Tale of the Strange City

Ethan and his family were taking a long road trip to another city. They lost their way and got diverted to a strange path. It led to a city where everybody falls asleep right at the moment when they feel sleepy and when they think, they think out loud.

What strange experiences do they face? How do they come out and find their way?

Draw here!

Q **Diverted:** *turn aside*

The Best friend Triangle

Lately Susan has started spending a lot of time with Linda, which was making Betty quite uncomfortable. She didn't want to act as a jealous best friend but inviting Linda to their slumber party was just too much.

How will Betty react? Will Susan and Betty continue to be best friends?

Struggles & troubles

The Football Tournament

Tiffany had to prove herself. Everybody had made fun of her that she cannot be a successful football player and should go to a dancing club instead. But she knew she had it in her. Today was the big day of the football tournament. Just before the match kicked off, she found out that her shoe was torn.

What does she do now? Does she win in the end?

The Last Goodbyes

Molly had never thought that she would have to leave this neighborhood which was like a family. She couldn't imagine a single day without seeing Ashley and Tristin. But dad has found a job way better than the current one, so they have to shift from this city.

How will Ashley and Tristin react to this news? How are they going to spend the last few days? Will they ever meet in the future? Will Molly make new friends?

Trekking Trouble

The summer camp that Linda had joined, arranged a mountain trekking tour with twenty girls, four adults incharge, a nurse and a guide. Suddenly, the girls start to get too sick to walk for some unknown reason. Going back is equally risky, as the phone signals are down.

What do they do? How do they get out of this situation and reach their camp safely?

Draw here!

The mistaken friendship

Mom was always against the idea of me spending time with Stephanie, for reasons I was always unable to understand. For me she was the smartest and the most fun person to spend time with. Until one day, I was proven wrong.

From Rich to Poor

Della was among the elite of the town and went to a school which most kids could only dream about. She had two nannies to look after her. But since the start of this year, her father's business was going downhill to the extent that they had to sell the house and shift into a small apartment.

Downhill: *fall*   **Extent:** *level*   **Nannies:** *childcarer*

Catching the fraud

Sam and Tracy worked hard all summers for a charity group that collects and sells old stuff to provide food and clothes for the needy. But lately they started to suspect the honesty of the group leader. When they dig more about this, they uncover a big fraud.

Draw here!

Fraud: cheating   **Suspect:** doubt

Burgular in the neighborhood

I was bored and exhausted and was just sitting by the window, observing the peaceful afternoon in our neighborhood, when suddenly I started noticing a quiet chaos in Jennifer's house. In a few minutes, I realized that they were being robbed by the burglars.

What should you do?

Draw here!

Ten Thousand dollars Cash prize

Amy had worked hard for the Science project, but still she didn't expect to win any position in that world wide competition. Above all, the ten thousand cash prize was a total surprise for her.

What will she do with all that money?

From the Jungle to the City

A girl has lived in the jungle all her life with her parents. Now because of new orders from the council of forests and nature, the whole forest is being vacated for some unknown reasons. The family has shifted to a small town where everything is shockingly new for her.

Write about her experience.

🔍 **Council:** *committee*   **Vacate:** *leave*

The Burdensome Secret

Janet was Molly's next door neighbor and her good friend. They would stand and wait at the bus stop together. One day Janet told her something important and asked her to keep it as a secret. According to it, Janet was in trouble and if the secret was out, she would be in more trouble.

What will Molly do? What was the secret? Will Janet come out of trouble?

Burdensome: *weighty / troublesome*

Protest for the Neighborhood

Henry's neighborhood is being demolished to make way for a huge government project. How does he protest and gather people to talk to the mayor of the town?

Draw here!

Demolished: *destroyed* **Protest:** *challenge*

From Janitor to Psychologist

John always wished to be a psychologist. He liked to study people and their behaviours. He had always wished to be one of the students who come to study such subjects in college where currently he was only a janitor with no money. Little did he know that he would find a way and one day become a well-known psychologist.

Escape from Orphanage

. He always thought he was the most useless creature on earth. He would look in the mirror for a noticeably long time to pick out some reason for the bad treatment he gets from the orphanage wardens. Lately, he has been working on his plan to escape.

The Silver Vase

Cindy broke the most precious belonging her mother had always protected; the silver vase given to her grandfather by the Mayor of the town as a token of appreciation for his efforts during the famine. Cindy knows that panicking will only worsen the situation and therefore thinks of a plan to get hold of a similar-looking vase.

The Worker of the Pyramids

The boy lives in times of Pharaoh when the pyramids were being built. His mother had died when he was a baby. His father had taken care of him with love and affection. He has reached the age when soldiers have started forcing the boys to carry the heavy loads for construction. He is too weak for such heavy duty.

Draw here!

Affection: *love*

Visit to the Castle

Emma always went to the meadow beside a huge old tree, not far from their family farm, whenever she needed some time alone with herself. She met princess Olivia there, who used to come for similar reasons. They became friends immediately. Princess Olivia invites Emma to her castle one day.

How does that go?

Draw here!

Meadow: *field*

Trapped in the Prison

Daniel is stuck in the enemy's prison for the last two months; that is a year after he joined the military as a soldier. He misses his five year old daughter and his loving wife.

How long does he have to stay in the prison? What are his feelings?

Draw here!

The lost letter of the Queen

It was feared that a war was about to break out. The most responsible knight was sent by the queen with a very urgent message to the other kingdom. But in the middle of their four-day journey, the knight lost the letter on his way.

How does he take care of the matter?

The Great Invention

We had planned everything together to build a car that runs on solar energy, Charlotte had come up with a detailed plan to get all the resources. Lucy was our scientist, she knew every technical detail there was to know. Helen and I were responsible for all the arrangements but none of us expected what happened in the end.

Draw here!

Technical: *scienftific / practical*

Visit to another Planet

David had hidden his alien friend Oolam in his closet for a month now. He was requested by the alien to keep his presence a secret. Now Oolam was offering David to go with him to his planet for a week. He promised to freeze the time so that David's parents will never know. What will David do?

What will David do?

Draw here!

Shrunk to an Inch

There was this cool looking gadget in dad's study, where Ava wasn't allowed to go. But today he wasn't home and she needed the stapler for some work. She pressed random buttons on the gadget and now she was shrunk down to one inch for an hour.

What would she do?

Draw here!

Invention of Trouble

A scientist was working on the tiniest particle of matter when one thing led to another and he invented a disastrous weapon by coincidence. One of the government officials found out and now the scientist is offered a huge amount of money for it.

Should he accept the offer? What happens when he accepts or declines?

Coincidence: *chance*

Into the Future

During his trip to China, Ryan went inside an old souvenir shop where he found a unique mirror with buttons on it. He didn't pay a lot of attention to it and forgot all about it until one day when he was packing his stuff, he found it. Pressed some buttons and looked in the mirror for one minute. Now, he is teleported fifty years ahead in future.

What does he see?

Souvenir: *token/reminder*   **Teleported:** *fast travel between two locations*

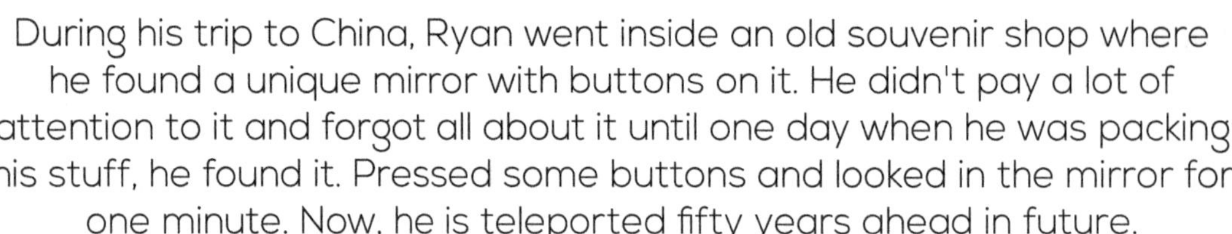

Ahead of Time

Noah is asked by a secret agent company to undergo a surgery after which he will have extra powers to see the other person's action 5 minutes prior to when the other person actually performs it.

Will he undergo the surgery? How will it be used by the agency? What will be his mission?

Q **Undergo:** *go through*

The Speaking Computer

Bella was using her computer for the research assignment her teacher had given. Suddenly,t her computer starts speaking to her as if there is a person is sitting inside it.

What should she do? Should she tell her parents?

My Secret Ingredient

You have invented a secret pasta recipe which is getting famous overnight. What are it's secret ingredients and do you share the recipe?

Haircut gone wrong

You went for a haircut, the barber accidentally shaved a strip of your hair. You have to attend your elder sister's wedding the next day. Do you hide it or accept it? What is everybody's reaction?

Draw here!

The Lonely Man

You are a delivery boy for a fast-food restaurant. What kind of people do you meet?
You made a friend, who orders twice a week and lives alone. What is his story?

Younger to Older

You went to space with the speed of light, when you came back, you find out that
your younger sister has turned into an old lady and you are even younger than you
used to be. How would you react?

Draw here!

A Believable Robot

You are given a robot. You have to give him a personality so it blends with other kids as well. What kind of a robot will it be?

The Giant Sister

Your sister's face and body starts growing larger and larger by the minute. What do you do?

Draw here!

Upside down Life

Imagine you wake up into a world where parents had to go to school and kids had to look after the house and arrange food. What is the routine of the day?

Short Stories

A delicious Challenge

You have entered a secret door. The place is filled with your favorite food. But if you eat it your life will fast forward ten years and you will never be able to know what happened in those ten years. What is that food? Did you eat it? What will happen if you do?

Draw here!

Meeting my Ideal

You are traveling in an aeroplane, and the person sitting next to you is your favorite famous person. It's a long flight. Who is that person? How do you interact?

The running Matchsticks

You were playing with the matchsticks and the matchsticks started running all over the place with flame on. How did you prevent the matchsticks from burning the house down?

Draw here!

Meeting my Favorite Character

You are allowed to meet any character from any book that you like, who would you meet? What would you say?

Draw here!

Interviewing my Parents

Strangely, you have turned into a reporter who is going to interview your parents about something important. You are allowed to ask anything and yet they won't find out it is you. What would you ask?

Captain Scammer

You're a pirate in a huge pirate cruise ship. You get to know about the evil plans of your captain who plans to get hold of all the treasures himself and kill half of the crew. How do you save your fellows?

Draw here!

Saving a troubled Pet

You volunteer and register yourself for the troubled pet center. You are allowed to choose a pet. You can either choose a snake, a lizard or an alligator. What would you choose? How would you keep it?

Identical but not Twins?

You found an adult, with identical childhood pictures as yours, same experiences and stories to share. How do you react? What is the secret behind it?

____

____

____

____

____

____

____

The Time Capsule

You and your friend found a time capsule in your friends house while planting seeds in the backyard. It is a hundred years old. What do you find in it? There is a letter. What does it say?

____

____

____

Draw here!

____

____

____

Principal for a Day

According to some strange law set by the school, you are made the principal of the school for one day. What changes will you bring? What new rules will you make?

Chaos in the Quiet

You are in the library. It is very quiet. You are using the computer. Suddenly, the sound system is broken and full volume is on. No matter which key you press it doesn't turn off. What do you experience and how does it end?